MY BODY Inside and Out!

My Amazing Sense of Taste

by Ruth Owen

Consultant:

Suzy Gazlay, MA
Recipient, Presidential Award for Excellence in Science Teaching

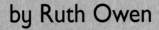

Ruby Tuesday Books

Published in 2014 by Ruby Tuesday Books Ltd.

Copyright © 2014 Ruby Tuesday Books Ltd.

Editor: Mark J. Sachner
Designer: Emma Randall
Production: John Lingham

Photo credits:
Ruby Tuesday Books: 11 (bottom), 14; Science Photo
Library: 9; Shutterstock: Cover, 1, 4–5, 6–7, 8, 11 (top),
12–13, 15, 16–17, 18–19, 20–21, 23.

Library of Congress Control Number: 2013919034

ISBN 978-1-909673-38-0

Printed and published in the United States of America

For further information including rights and permissions
requests, please contact our Customer Service Department
at 877-337-8577.

Contents

Good Tastes, Bad Tastes 4

Get Ready to Taste 6

Check Out Your Tongue 8

Thousands of Taste Buds 10

Different Flavors 12

Tasty Messages 14

Your Nose Helps, Too! 16

Cold, Hot, and Painful! 18

Keep On Tasting! 20

Glossary 22

Index 24

Read More 24

Learn More Online 24

Words shown in **bold** in the text are
explained in the glossary.

Good Tastes, Bad Tastes

Think about how good a juicy apple or your favorite ice cream flavor tastes.

Now think about how horrible a sip of milk tastes when the milk has gone bad.

Every time you eat or drink something, your **sense** of taste is hard at work.

It helps you enjoy the food and drink that you put into your mouth.

It can also warn you that the taste of something isn't right and could make you ill.

How exactly does your sense of taste work, though? Let's check it out!

You have five senses that help keep you safe and help you enjoy your world. Your five senses are seeing, hearing, smelling, tasting, and touching.

Not everyone likes the same tastes. You might like a food that your best friend hates.

5

Get Ready to Taste

When it's time to eat or drink, your senses go into action.

Before you even take a bite, you see the food and smell it.

This makes your mouth start producing a slimy liquid called **saliva**, or spit.

Once the food is in your mouth, your teeth cut and chew it into small pieces.

Then your tongue works with your teeth to mix the chewed-up food with saliva.

As your tongue helps mash up the food, it **detects** the food's flavors.

You use your senses of sight and smell to get information about food.

Your teeth and
tongue mash up
your food.

Your tongue is made up
of lots of small **muscles**.
This hardworking body
part helps you talk, eat,
and taste your food.

Check Out Your Tongue

If you could look at your tongue under a **microscope**, what would you see?

You would see that your tongue is covered with thousands of tiny bumps called **papillae**.

Some papillae are shaped like cones.

Their job is to grip food and help move it around in your mouth.

Other papillae have rounded shapes.

These papillae contain **taste buds** that help you taste your food.

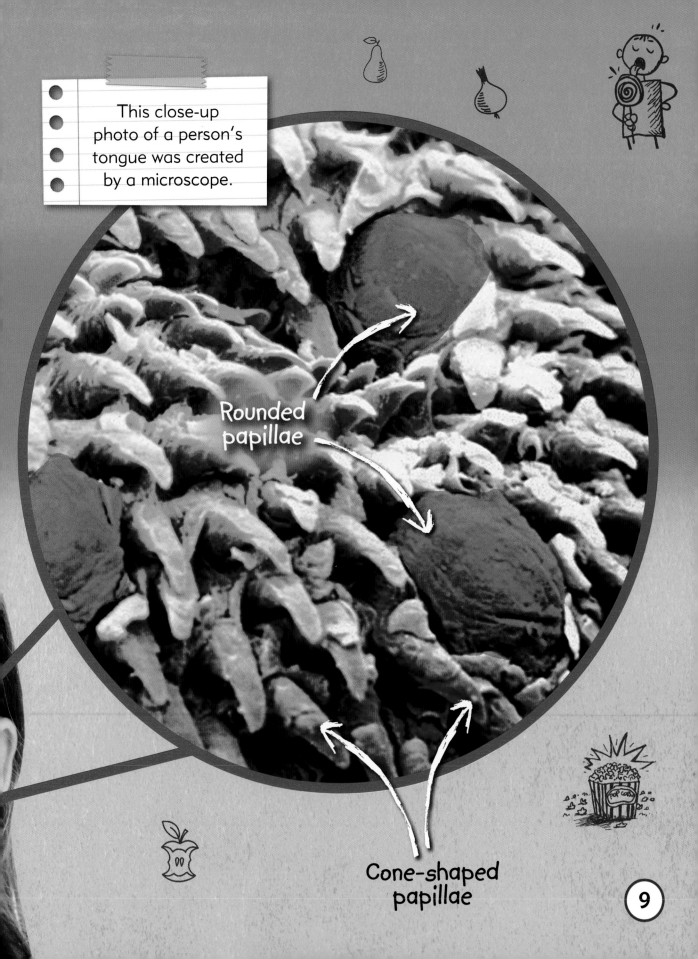

This close-up photo of a person's tongue was created by a microscope.

Rounded papillae

Cone-shaped papillae

Thousands of Taste Buds

The tiny papillae on your tongue contain about 10,000 taste buds.

Each **microscopic** taste bud is made up of tiny parts called **cells**.

The cells fit together like the sections of an orange.

On each taste bud there are lots of hairs.

These hairs touch the tiny pieces of mashed-up food in your saliva.

Then the hairs detect what type of flavor the food has.

You also have some taste buds on the roof of your mouth and at the back of your throat.

This picture shows what a taste bud looks like.

Tiny pieces of food

Hairs

Cells

Saliva

11

Different Flavors

All the different foods you eat can be sorted into five different types of flavors.

The five flavors are sweet, salty, sour, bitter, and umami.

Different groups of taste buds detect each different type of flavor.

The taste buds on the tip of your tongue detect sweet flavors such as chocolate and honey.

The taste buds in the middle of your tongue detect umami flavors such as meat and cheese.

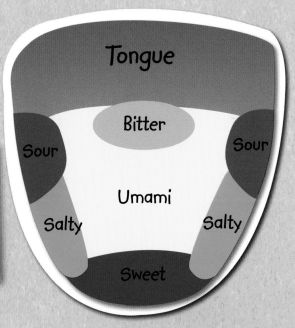

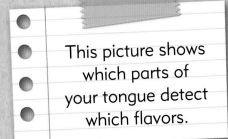

This picture shows which parts of your tongue detect which flavors.

Sour

Grapes

Lemons

Grapefruit

Bitter

Coffee

Unsweetened cocoa

Red cabbage

Umami

Meat

Cheese

Mushrooms

Salty

Popcorn

Potato chips

A pretzel

A lemon ice pop has a sour flavor.

Sweet

Ice cream

Chocolate

Honey

Tasty Messages

As you chew a mouthful of food, your taste buds are hard at work detecting flavors.

Once a taste bud has gathered the information it needs, it sends a message to your brain.

The message travels along a pathway of cells called **nerve cells**.

The message tells your brain if the food has a sweet, salty, sour, bitter, or umami flavor.

Your brain receives the message and, in an instant, you taste the flavor.

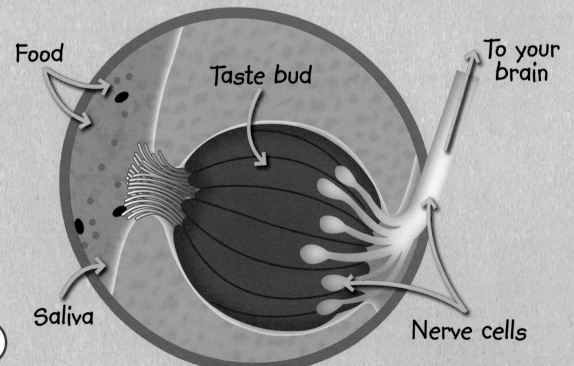

Food

Taste bud

To your brain

Saliva

Nerve cells

Brain

Your brain receives the message from your taste buds that the food has a sweet flavor.

Your brain tells you that the food tastes sweet.

Mmmmmmmmm. Sweet!

Your Nose Helps, Too!

It's not just your taste buds that help you taste your food.

Your nose and sense of smell help, too.

Your nose smells your food even before you put it into your mouth.

Once you are chewing your food, more smells travel from your mouth up into your nose.

Special cells in your nose collect information from the smells and send messages to your brain.

These messages also help you taste your food.

Sometimes when you have a cold, you can't taste your food. Your taste buds are working, but your blocked nose can't smell to do its job.

Your taste buds can tell what type of flavor food has. To figure out what the food is, though, your taste buds, nose, and brain must work together.

Your taste buds tell your brain the food has a sweet flavor.

+

Your nose sends information about the food's smell to your brain.

=

Your brain puts it altogether and figures out that the sweet-flavored food is watermelon.

Cold, Hot, and Painful!

Your tongue doesn't only taste your food, it also uses touch to tell you about your food.

As your tongue touches ice cream, cells in the papillae detect that the food is cold.

Your tongue can also detect when food is hot.

This information about your food is sent to your brain along nerve cells.

Then your brain lets you feel that the food is cold or hot.

Feeling the temperature of your food helps you enjoy it, and keeps you from hurting your mouth.

Your tongue also lets you feel if your food is rough or smooth.

Your tongue has cells that detect if something is hurting it. These cells send warning messages to your brain. Then your brain makes you feel pain so you stop doing what you're doing.

When you eat food that contains spicy-hot chili peppers, your tongue feels like it's burning. That feeling is your brain making you feel pain. The burning pain warns you that the peppers are hurting your tongue!

19

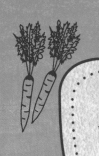

Keep On Tasting!

Your sense of taste is very important.

If something tastes bad, it helps warn you that the food or drink might harm you.

It also makes eating a lot of fun because you get to enjoy many different flavors.

As you become an adult, you will have fewer taste buds than you do today.

This means that foods you don't like now might not taste so strong as you grow up.

So never stop trying out new foods with your amazing sense of taste!

Your taste buds die and regrow about every two weeks. As you get older, some of your taste buds don't regrow, so foods taste different.

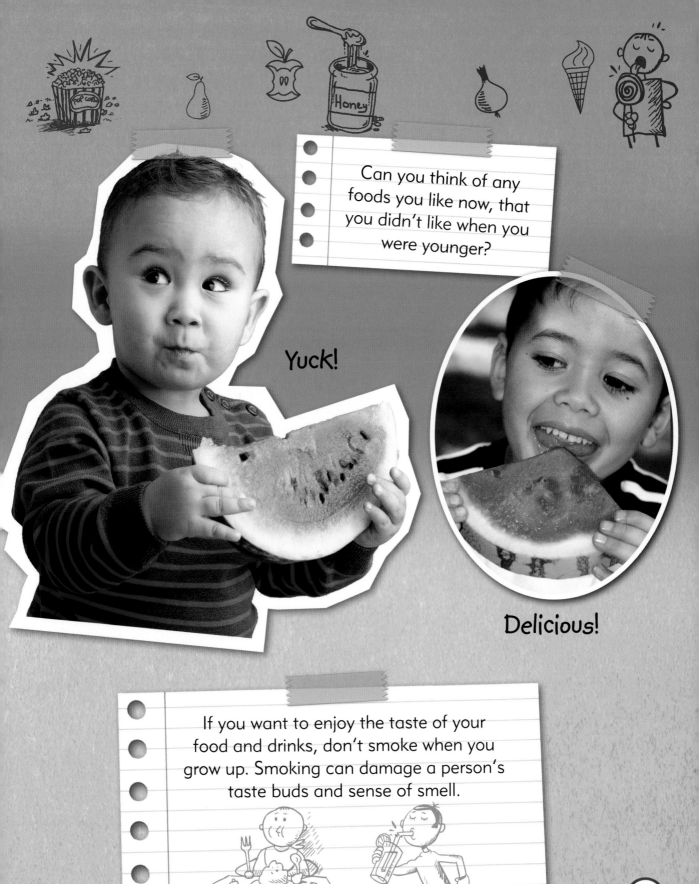

Can you think of any foods you like now, that you didn't like when you were younger?

Yuck!

Delicious!

If you want to enjoy the taste of your food and drinks, don't smoke when you grow up. Smoking can damage a person's taste buds and sense of smell.

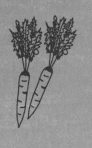

Glossary

cells (SELZ)
Very tiny parts of a living thing. Your bones, muscles, skin, hair, and every part of you are made of cells.

detect (dee-TECT)
To recognize or identify something.

microscope (MIKE-ruh-skope)
A tool or machine that is used to see things that are too small for a person to see with his or her eyes.

microscopic (mike-roh-SKAH-pik)
So small that it can only be seen with a microscope.

muscle (MUH-suhl)
A part of the body that contracts, or tightens up, and then relaxes to produce movement. Muscles use energy that comes from food.

nerve cell (NURV SEL)
One of the billions of tiny cells that carry information between your brain and other parts of your body.

papillae (puh-PIL-ee)
Tiny bumps on your tongue that help you grip your food and move it around in your mouth. Your taste buds are positioned on the papillae on your tongue.

saliva (suh-LY-vuh)
A liquid in the mouth that helps us chew, taste, and swallow.

sense (SENSS)
One of the five ways that you collect information about the world around you. Your senses are seeing, hearing, smelling, tasting, and touching.

taste bud (TAYST BUHD)
A group of cells on your tongue that detects the flavors in your food. Your taste buds send information about the flavors to your brain so that you can taste your food.

23

Index

B
bitter flavors 12–13, 14
brain 14–15, 16–17,
    18–19

C
cells 10–11, 14, 16,
    18–19
colds 16

F
flavors 4, 6, 10, 12–13,
    14–15, 17, 20

H
hairs (on taste buds)
    10–11

M
microscopes 8–9
muscles 7

N
nerve cells 14–15, 18
noses 16–17

P
pain 19
papillae 8–9, 10, 18

S
saliva 6, 10–11, 14
salty flavors 12–13, 14
seeing 5, 6
senses 4–5, 6

smelling 5, 6, 16–17, 21
smoking 21
sour flavors 12–13, 14
sweet flavors 12–13,
    14–15, 17

T
taste buds 8, 10–11, 12,
    14–15, 16–17, 20–21
teeth 6–7
tongues 6–7, 8–9, 10,
    12, 18–19
touching 5, 18

U
umami flavors 12–13, 14

Read More

Hewitt, Sally.
*Tastes good! (Let's Start
Science)*. New York: Crabtree
Publishing Company (2008).

Rissman, Rebecca.
Tasting (The Five Senses).
North Mankato, MN:
Heinemann-Raintree (2010).

Learn More Online

To learn more about your sense of taste, go to
www.rubytuesdaybooks.com/mybodytaste